# What is the Church?

Mandy Groce and Bill Bell

Illustrated by Tessa Janes

ISBN: 978-1-84550-703-9
Published in 2011 and reprinted in 2016
by Christian Focus Publications,
Geanies House, Fearn, Tain, Ross-shire,
IV20 1TW, Scotland, U.K.

Text by Mandy Groce and Bill Bell
Illustrations by Tessa Janes
Cover design by Daniel van Straaten
Printed in China



sojourn
COMMUNITY CHURCH

CF4•K
*Because you're never too young to know Jesus*

But you are a chosen people, a royal priesthood, a holy nation, a people belonging to God, that you may declare the praises of him who called you out of darkness into his wonderful light. Once you were not a people, but now you are the people of God; once you had not received mercy, but now you have received mercy.

1 Peter 2:9-10 (NIV)

*What Is The Church?* was written to teach preschool children that the church is not a building. It is a people that God has called together and made alive by faith. Unlike other books on the church, this book does not answer the question by first telling about the activities that the church does (gathering, preaching, communion, baptism, counseling, discipline) – although those things are essential marks of the church and they should not be ignored. Instead, this book begins with who God's people are – recognizing that the church's activity results from its identity. When we call children to be a part of the church, we are calling them to be a part of a gospel people. And, as a gospel people, the church is a believing family, a community of missionaries, servants, learners, and worshipers. At Sojourn, we call our people to stop going to church and to start being the church. Once God's people know who they are, we can challenge them to be who they are. In other words, we call them to live as the people that God has made them to be.

Jared Kennedy
Pastor for Children's and Parent Ministries
Sojourn Community Church, Louisville, KY

This book belongs to:

Let's say you ask me, "What's the church?"
I'd say, "Not what, but WHO!"
The church is made of people just
like me and just like you.

The church is not a place we go
to meet on special days.
It's us—it's he and she and we—
called out to bring Christ praise.

Christ died and rose to life again
to wipe away our sin.
This good news makes us people,
who love and trust in Him.

# FAMILY

God's church is built of human hearts—
Men, women, girls, and boys.
By faith we're made God's family.
Together we rejoice!

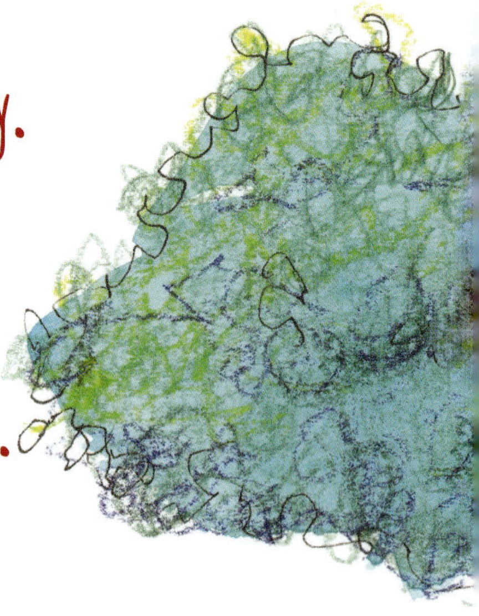

We all are like an orphan child.
Our sin makes us alone.
Through Jesus, we're adopted in
and treasured as God's own.

# MISSIONARIES

We're missionaries—ALL the church!—
who go to serve and preach.
We love no matter who the soul
and help those in our reach.
Sometimes we travel far to reach
the needy, lost, and poor.
At other times we do the same
for those who live next door.

# SERVANTS

Like Jesus came to humbly serve,
the church serves those in need.
We work and care for those who hurt;
those hungry we will feed.

We are no longer slaves to sin.
Now we are free to give!
God's love for people flows through us
in how we daily live.

# LEARNERS

To learn of God in all his ways,
is not a task or chore.
It's truly joy to seek God's Word,
to know him more and more.

We study deeply in God's Word.
We think and memorize.
It's in the Bible that we find
Christ is our greatest prize.

You see, the Bible isn't just
a myth or fairy tale.
This book speaks truth of Jesus Christ.
His words will never fail.

# WORSHIPERS

We strive to live with thankful hearts
that give our Father praise.
We worship him with all we do,
boast only in his ways.
I know it may seem like a lot,
but in these many things
the church is giving praise to Christ,
our risen Lord and King.

That's why we serve and learn and preach
and care and help and give.
We love because he first loved us.
He died that we might live.

So...
Let's say I ask you, "What's the church?"
Just say, "Not what, but WHO!"
For now you know the church is NOT
A building you can view.

God's church is not a place we go
to learn and pray and sing.
It's WE who are the church through faith
in Jesus as our King.

Teaching our children is a precious responsibility, one that requires that we have a biblical view of God's church. Contemporary conversation tends to keep us referring to the church as a structure, but we hope that this book and the discussion questions below encourage you and your children to more fully understand WHO the church is as a people.

The Truth:

- The church is God's people.
- God's church includes every faithful believer in Christ, throughout time and across the world.
- We are special because of Jesus' gift of faith to us.
- We don't have to earn our membership in the church.

## Discussion Questions for You and Your Child:

- When you talk about church, do you usually talk about people or a place?
- How do people become part of God's church?
- Do we have to do anything or be anything extraordinary to join God's church family?

## Activities to solidify your child's understanding of who the church is:

- Create a "family tree" with pictures or drawings of your local church family.
- Make up a song together about being the church.
- Make a collage of drawings or cut-outs showing ways that the church shows itself in your family's life.

Christian Focus Publications publishes books for adults and children under its four main imprints: Christian Focus, CF4K, Mentor and Christian Heritage. Our books reflect our conviction that God's Word is reliable and Jesus is the way to know him, and live for ever with him.

Our children's publication list includes a Sunday School curriculum that covers pre-school to early teens, and puzzle and activity books. We also publish personal and family devotional titles, biographies and inspirational stories that children will love.

If you are looking for quality Bible teaching for children then we have an excellent range of Bible stories and age-specific theological books.

From pre-school board books to teenage apologetics, we have it covered!

Find us at our web page:
www.christianfocus.com

CF4K
Because you're never too young to know Jesus